Introduction to Ethical Investing in India

By Siva Prasad Bose and Joy Bose

Published by Joy Bose

Copyright © 2023 Joy Bose

Contents

Dedication

This book is dedicated to all the companies in India who subscribe to ethical values and sustainable goals.

Preface

Ethical investing, also called by different names such as Environmental Social and Governance (ESG) investing, responsible investing, mindful investing and sustainable investing, has recently become more popular. Investors, particularly younger investors, are getting more concerned over the wider social and other impact of their investments and wish to contribute to positive changes in the world, rather than contribute towards increasing suffering. The highs and lows of the stock markets in different countries further give a push towards ethical investing as a strategy to identify more stable companies that believe in ethical and sustainable values and which are, therefore, more likely to be profitable in the long term.

In this book, we introduce the concept of ethical investing and consider the avenues by which investors can invest ethically within India today. We discuss green energy, various ESG and ethical mutual funds and social investing avenues.

It is hoped that this book will raise awareness towards ethical investing and inspire existing and prospective investors to invest in a way that uses their money towards the wider good in this world.

Acknowledgements

In preparing this book, the authors would like to thank Vijay Sahu for his amazing investing course from the Siyona Academy, and Chetan Dhumane for their very helpful advice about investing.

Chapter 1: Introduction to Ethical Investing

In this chapter we discuss introduce the concept of ethical investing.

1.1 Definition of ethical investing

Ethical investing refers to the idea of investing in causes and organizations that are least ethically harmful, and most beneficial, to their employees, stakeholders and society as a whole, as well as generating a decent financial return for the investors. This may include investing in companies that contribute to the cause of education, environmental sustainability, public health, tackling inequality, tackling discrimination and other social evils and so on. It involves companies that subscribe to good corporate governance and labor practices, as well as those that are mindful and seek to minimize any harmful impact to the environment and wider society.

Alternative terms that may refer to ethical investing include responsible investing, sustainable investing and socially responsible investing. Such investments may be in various forms of investing such as stocks and bonds or other investment types such as real estate, as long as they are related to companies that meet the ethical standards and guidelines.

The management of such companies that are chosen for ethical investments should follow ethical practices generally as well as demonstrate a good standard of corporate governance.

1.2 Environmental Social and Governance (ESG) Criteria

They also refer to investing in company shares and mutual funds that follow environmental, social, and governance (ESG) criteria. Such criteria may include the following:

- **Environmental**: Greenhouse Gas Emissions, renewable energy, clean water, waste management, green buildings, climate change, pollution control, control of carbon emissions

- **Social**: corporate social responsibility, labor relations, privacy and data security, gender equality, social justice

- **Governance**: business ethics, independent board members, executive compensation, anti-corruption, treatment of minority shareholders,

Over time, use of such criteria by companies may result in long term profitability and improved operational performance.

1.3 ESG mutual funds

Recently there has been a rise in ESG based mutual funds in India, with many asset management companies and mutual fund houses coming up with their own ESG funds where people can invest.

Examples of ESG based mutual funds include SBI Magnum Equity ESG Fund, Tata ESG Fund, Axis ESG Equity fund, Kotak ESG Opportunities Fund, Quantum India ESG Equity Fund and so on.

1.4 S&P BSE 100 ESG Index

The S&P BSE 100 ESG Index is an index of companies which is designed to measure securities that meet sustainability investing criteria while maintaining a risk and performance profile similar to the S&P BSE 100.

The methodology followed by the ESG index excludes companies working in areas involving controversial weapons, thermal coal, tobacco products, oil sands, small arms, and military contracting. There are also exclusions based on the United Nations Global Compact (UNGC).

One can get more information about this ESG index at: https://www.spglobal.com/spdji/en/indices/esg/sp-bse-100-esg-index.

Other ESG based Indian Indexes include the following:

- S&P BSE Greenex

- S&P BSE Carbonex

- NIFTY 100 ESG Index

- NIFTY 100 Enhanced ESG Index

1.5 MSCI Indian ESG Leaders Index

The MSCI India ESG Leaders Index is a capitalization weighted index that provides exposure to companies with high Environmental, Social and Governance (ESG) performance relative to their sector peers. MSCI India ESG Leaders Index consists of large and mid-cap companies in Indian markets.

More information about this ESG index can be seen at https://www.msci.com/our-solutions/indexes/esg-indexes

1.6 Companies working in ESG sectors

There is also a surge in interest in startups and established listed and unlisted companies working in ESG related sectors such as renewable energy, green technology, agritech, solar energy, waste management, electric vehicles and e-mobility. The number of startups and investments by venture capitalists in such sectors are also rising, combined with increased incentives by the Indian government for companies in such sectors.

1.7 UN Sustainable Development Goals

Ethical investing may also refer to any investment that helps in one of the United Nations Sustainable Development Goals (SDG), which include No Poverty, Zero Hunger, Good Health and Well-being, Quality Education, Gender Equality, Clean Water and Sanitation, Affordable and Clean Energy, Decent Work and Economic Growth, Industry, Innovation and Infrastructure, Reduced Inequalities, Sustainable Cities and Communities, Responsible Consumption and Production, Climate Action, Life Below Water, Life On Land, Peace, Justice and Strong Institutions, and Partnerships for the Goals.

1.8 Shariah Compliant Investing

Other definitions of ethical investing include investing in companies that are compliant to religious and ethical codes such as the Islamic Shariah.

Some of the criteria for being compliant to shariah Islamic law include: Shariah prohibits income from alcohol, abusive drugs, pork products, gambling, weapons, etc. Shariah also forbids investment in companies that earn most of their income from interest or Riba.

1.9 Corporate Social Responsibility (CSR) Guidelines

The Indian Government Ministry of Corporate Affairs published a number of Corporate Social Responsibility (CSR) guidelines in 2009. These include six core elements, around which companies are encouraged to form a CSR policy. These core elements include the following:

- Care for stakeholders

- Proper functioning

- Respect for workers' rights and welfare

- Respect for human rights

- Respect for the environment

- Activities for social and inclusive development.

1.10 Types of Ethical investing

Ethical investing can be in any of the following forms, besides others:

- Investing in Environmental Social and Governance (ESG) mutual funds

- Investing in Sharia compliant funds

- Investing in green energy

- Investing in social investing and social finance platforms

In the following chapters we will discuss each of them in more detail.

12

1.11 Conclusion

In this chapter, we have discussed the meaning and types of ethical investing.

Chapter 2: Advantages of ethical investing

In this chapter, we discuss the advantages of ethical investing.

2.1 Long term stability and growth

One of the advantages of ethical investing is that companies that follow good ethical standards are more likely to be stable companies that produce good value for their shareholders and wider stakeholders, and thus are worthy of investing in the long run. These tend to be more stable and have lower risk.

2.2 Alignment with ethical values

Also, some investors may prefer to invest mainly in companies that align with their ethical values. Since different investors may have different kinds of preferences on what is ethical, there is no single rule to identify ethical companies. However, some guidelines, such as those related to environment and society, may be common for most people.

2.3 Quotes about ethical investing from experts

Following are some quotes about ethical investing from a few investment experts:

"Investing is not only about making money. It's also about doing well. And the most successful investors are those who understand the issues that matter and make well-informed investment

decisions." - Jeremy Grantham, famed value investor and chief investment strategist of GMO, one of the first persons to start an index fund in the 1970s.

"Investing in companies that are part of the solution to the world's sustainability challenges is not only the right thing to do, it's also the smart thing to do." - David Blood, founding partner of Generation Investment Management.

"Investors need to incorporate environmental, social and governance (ESG) factors into their decision-making processes, not only to be responsible corporate citizens, but because they can have a material impact on financial performance." - Mary Schapiro, 29th Chair of the U.S. Securities and Exchange Commission (SEC).

"Ethical investing is not just about avoiding problematic companies. It's about investing in companies that are trying to create a better world." - Audrey Choi, CEO of Morgan Stanley's Institute for Sustainable Investing.

"The financial case for ESG investing is strong. Companies that rank highly on ESG metrics tend to be better managed, have lower risk, and generate better long-term financial returns." - John Goldstein, Managing Director, Head of the Sustainable Finance Group, Goldman Sachs Asset Management.

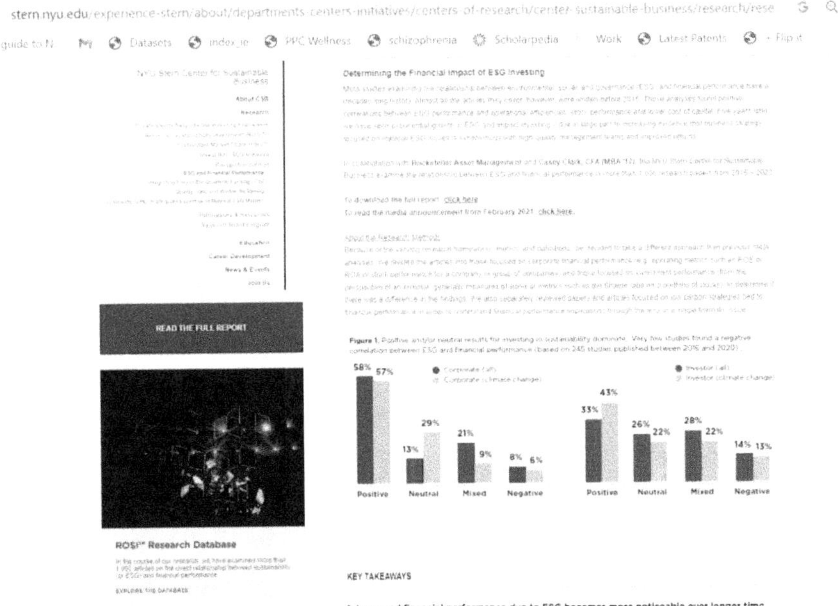

Figure: Screenshot from the Stern report showing a positive correlation between ESG and financial performance

2.4 Research on the benefits from ESG investing

The NYU Stern Center for Sustainable Business and Rockefeller Asset Management, wrote a research report on the relationship between ESG and financial performance after studying research papers written on the topic. It found a positive relationship between ESG and financial performance in 58% of their studied 1000 research papers about performance of companies (written between 2015 to 2020), that focused on operational metrics such as ROE, ROA, or stock price, with only 8% showing a negative relationship. They also found that improved financial performance becomes more pronounced over longer timelines, ESG as a strategy performed better than negative screening approaches, and that it provided better protection during a downturn.

This shows that ethical or ESG oriented investing can not only make a positive impact on the world, but also generate better returns for investment in the longer term.

Reference:

https://www.stern.nyu.edu/experience-stern/about/departments-centers-initiatives/centers-of-research/center-sustainable-business/research/research-initiatives/esg-and-financial-performance

2.5 Conclusion

In this chapter we have discussed some of the advantages of ethical investing.

Chapter 3: Guidelines for ethical investing from different religions

In this chapter, we discuss some guidelines for ethical investing taken from different religions. We can leverage the timeless wisdom from different religions in building an ethical approach to investing.

3.1 Jewish guidelines

Jewish guidelines for ethical investing include the following:

- **Tzedakah or righteousness**: charity, preferably in places where donor helps the recipient to become self-supporting.

- **Tikkun olam or repair the world**: invest in social / environment friendly companies or orgs.

- **Tzedek or justice and fairness**: invest in companies with a commitment to social impact, combating inequality etc.

- **G'milut chasadim or lovingkindness, caring and compassion**: invest in places which support the needy, sick and elderly.

- **Tikya or hope**: invest in places that inspire people and give hope to the world.

Reference: https://thejewishnews.com/2020/09/09/a-jewish-approach-to-planning-and-investing/

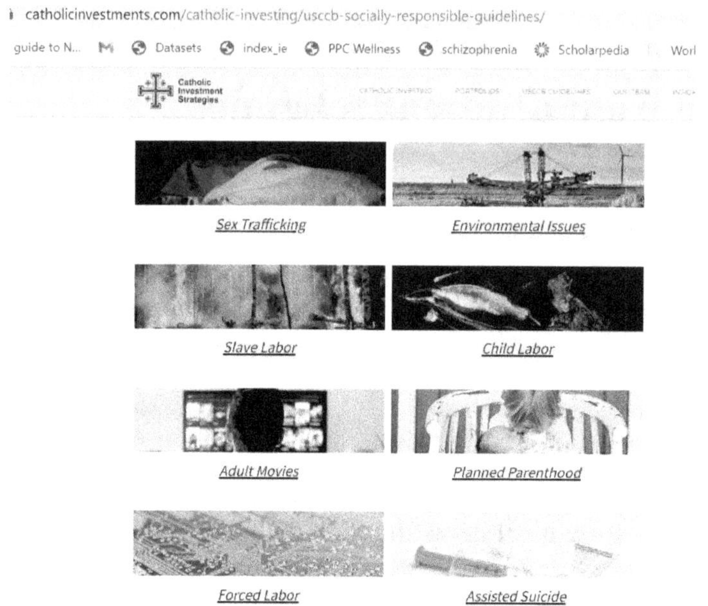

Figure: Screenshot of a website discussing catholic investment strategies for ethical investing

3.2 Catholic guidelines

Catholic guidelines for ethical investing include the following:

- Avoid evil, meaning do not invest in places that promote morally questionable actions such as pornography, racial and gender discrimination, arms production, stem cell research, abortion, slave labor, child labor, predatory lending and so on.

- Do good, meaning to invest in places that work towards protecting human life and dignity, economic justice, environment and encourage corporate responsibility. Also, be active shareholders and take an interest in the policies of the companies where you invest, attend and vote in the shareholder meetings and actively work to improving the company policies.

Reference: https://www.catholicinvestments.com/catholic-investing/usccb-socially-responsible-guidelines/

3.3 Islamic guidelines for Shariah compliant investing

The Holy Quran prohibits interest or **Riba**, views riba as an exploitative and unjust practice that harms individuals and society. It also encourages believers to donate money to needy people as Zaqat.

Quran in chapter 2, verse 275, states:

"Those who consume interest cannot stand [on the Day of Resurrection] except as one stands who is being beaten by Satan into insanity. That is because they say, "Trade is [just] like interest." But Allah has permitted trade and has forbidden interest. So whoever has received an admonition from his Lord and desists may have what is past, and his affair rests with Allah. But whoever returns to [dealing in interest or usury] - those are the companions of the Fire; they will abide eternally therein."

Hence, for Shariah compliant investing, companies and funds should not be getting most of their income from interest, rather than from the proceeds of honest business.

The Quran Chapter 30, verse 39 states:

"And whatever you give for interest to increase within the wealth of people will not increase with Allah. But what you give in zakah (charity), desiring the countenance of Allah - those are the multipliers."

Some shariah financial principles include the following:

- **Ijarah**, meaning giving an asset on rent or lease for the use of it, at a specific future period of time

- **Sukuk Bond** which is an Islamic bond that can generate returns to investors without being involved with Riba or interest.

One important idea is that the funds invested are deployed in carefully managed finance schemes and the profit earned is very close to the market rather than generated from speculation. It also involves avoiding investing in companies that make their money from the sale of alcohol, abusive drugs, pork products, gambling, weapons, and other such products.

Reference: https://taqwabanking.com/faqs.php

3.4 Buddhist guidelines (Sigalovada sutta)

According to the Buddha's teachings in Sigalovada sutta and other suttas, one needs to keep the following points in mind:

- One should be mindful of one's money, since it is a type of energy which can be both good or bad.

- Save aside money for times of need as well as invest in growing your business and career.

- Avoid vices that dissipate your wealth such as gambling and excessive greed

- Avoid cheating and lying and follow the precepts and moderation

- Do not be too attached to anything including money and profits.

Reference: https://buddhaweekly.com/the-secular-buddhist-approach-to-managing-money-wisely-as-taught-in-sutra/

3.5 Hinduism guidelines (Bhagavad Gita)

According to the principles in the karma yoga chapter of the Bhagavad Gita, the holy text of Hinduism:

- One should try and become a nishkaama or detached karma yogi, invest well after good research, work hard and honestly and get wealth.

- However, it is also important not to be attached too much to the fruits of one's work and the returns from one's investments.

- In short, do your homework before investing, but keep expectations realistic and do not fall into greed of getting high profits.

Reference: https://www.speakingtree.in/blog/bhagavad-gita-and-wealth-creation-626486

3.6 Conclusion

In this chapter we discussed some of the ethical guidelines about money and investing, which we can learn from the wisdom of different religions.

Chapter 4: General investing principles

In this chapter we discuss some general investing principles which experienced investors may know but beginning investors may not have experienced.

4.1 How much to invest and where

A good investor should have at least the following:

- A few months' worth of savings in a fixed deposit or FD for unforeseen emergencies.

- Put aside at least 10-20% of their disposable income each month in investing, whether in stocks, mutual funds, bonds, gold or other asset classes.

- Put aside some percentage of their salary each month towards retirement options such as Provident Funds (EPF and PPF) and Pension Schemes such as NPS.

- Have a good term insurance and health insurance policy at a minimum.

It is a good principle to put aside money for investment each month upon getting one's salary before paying for one's regular expenses like credit cards and groceries. The earlier one starts investing, the better returns one can get, since the money has more time to grow, because of the power of compounding.

One should do an analysis of their risk profile to know what kind of investor they are:

- Cautious investor: Keep more percentage of bonds and less of stocks in their portfolio

- Balanced investor: Keep a good mix of stocks and bonds and gold as per your age

- Aggressive investor: Mostly stocks and very less bonds.

The investing should be in a mixture of different classes: stocks, bonds, gold and real estate, and mutual funds.

One should also decide on how much to invest in different asset classes, as per their risk profile and age. The older one is and closer to retirement, the more they should invest in less risky options such as bonds and less in stocks. Therefore, when one is younger, one may decide to invest more into stocks and equity based mutual funds, while as one gets older one can go for a mix of stocks, bonds, equity and debt mutual funds, gold and other assets.

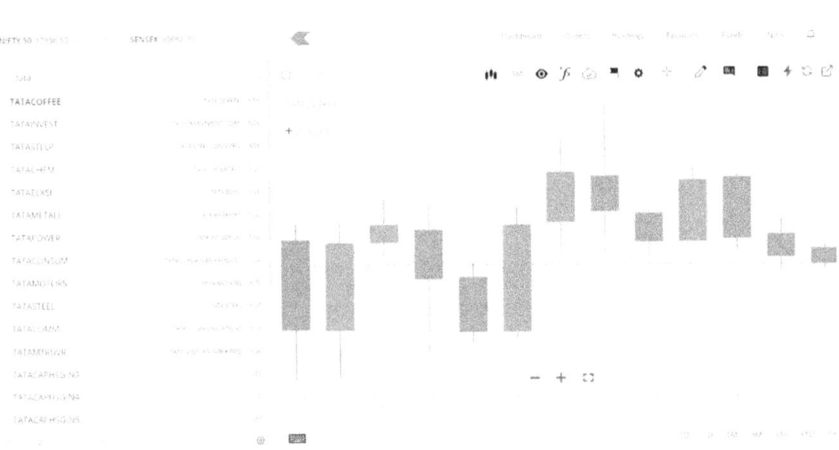

Figure: Screenshot from zerodha kite trading platform

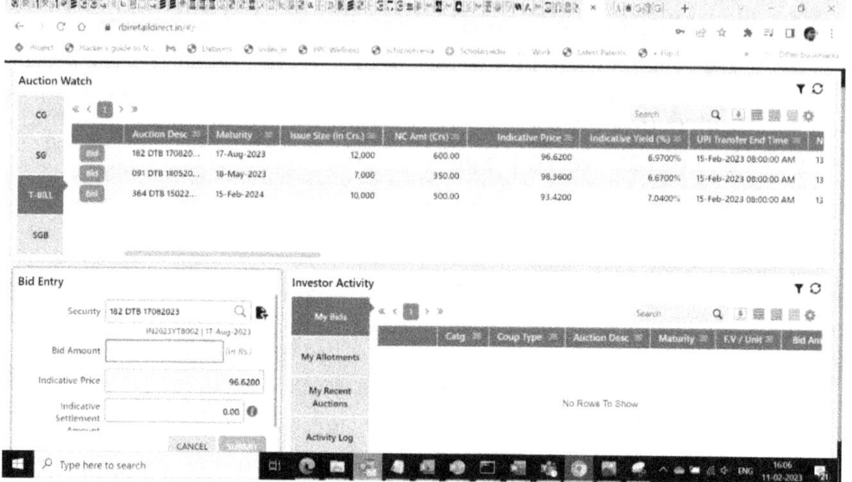

Figure: Screenshot from RBI retail direct website showing T bills

Some of the different investment options in India include the following:

- **Company shares, or stocks**, are the most common way to invest. They usually give good returns from appreciation in the value of the stock, as well as periodic dividends.

  To trade in shares, one can have a free account with an Indian stockbroker. Common stockbrokers include Zerodha, 5paisa, Upstox, Angel one, kotak securities, Motilal Oswal, groww, Sharekhan, Kotak Mahindra, ICICI Direct or any other broker. These may have different fees structures and value-added services, so one needs to carefully check these before enrolling.

  Out of these, Indmoney, vested, groww, indiainxga and a few other brokers give the option of investing in US and other foreign stocks as well, either by tying up with US based trading API providers such as Alpaca Securities or mainstream US brokers such as Interactive Brokers.

- **Mutual funds** are also a good way to invest, since they spread the risk from individual stocks. They have a huge variety and are available for different kinds of stocks, risk profiles, sectors etc.

There are bond or debt mutual funds, equities or stocks mutual funds, tracker funds, liquid funds and so on. Index fund or tracker funds track the whole sensex such as NSE and BSE sensex. They typically have a lower expense ratio and no exit load. NIFTY-50 and BSE Sensex are some of the main index funds based on the Indian stock markets. To guard against currency fall in value of rupee, one can similarly invest in US based index funds such as Vanguard's VTI, VOO, VT, Invesco's QQQ and so on.

Index funds are good for lower cost passive investing. Since the stock market usually grows in the long run, it is useful to invest a tracker fund such as NIFTY-50 either as a one time or SIP every month, and watch it grow over time and take advantage of the rising stock market.

Non-index funds, on the other hand, may be actively managed and have a higher cost in terms of expense ratio and exit load. But if the fund managers are experienced and from established fund management houses that have been around for a while (such as SBI mutual fund or Parag Parikh mutual fund), good at identifying which stocks to invest and been managing the fund well for the last few years, they may give higher returns.

One should also be careful when buying mutual funds which have made a huge profit very recently but not in earlier years. The best mutual funds are those that have been making consistent profits for a few years.

One can invest in mutual funds either by paying a one-time lumpsum, or by doing a SIP where one pays a fixed amount each month to buy the same mutual fund. SIP investing is a better way to guard against fluctuations in the value of the fund.

Mutual funds can be of two types: direct and regular. Regular mutual funds charge a little more commission than direct funds, but offered through third parties which may add value with services such as portfolio analysis and rebalancing. New fund offerings or NFOs are when a new mutual fund is launched, sometimes at a discount. Closed mutual funds have a closing date beyond which no new subscriptions are allowed, while open funds have no such restriction.

Mutual funds can be invested via one's stockbroker such as Zerodha coin or Samco RankMF or via dedicated curated mutual funds sites such as Scripbox and FundsIndia.

- **Bonds**, especially government bonds, are safer but also give lower returns, and are a good hedge against risks from stocks falling in value. One's portfolio should have a mix of stocks and bonds.

On the other hands, since the returns are fixed, bonds may lose money if there is high inflation, the Rupee falls in value compared to US dollar, or when the RBI interest rates rise.

There are two kinds of bonds, government bonds and corporate bonds. Government bonds or treasury bonds are typically the safest but may have lower returns than corporate bonds. When investing in corporate bonds, it is important to check the credit ratings of bonds (such as AAA or AA+). They can be bought from RBI retail direct website or broker sites like zerodha.

- **Gold** usually is inflation proof, i.e., it does not lose its value during inflation.

  One can invest in gold in different forms such as physical gold, digital gold (such as from MMTC PAMP website or apps such as Gullak gold app) and government's Sovereign Gold Bonds.

  However, one must beware of taxes such as GST on physical and digital gold, which is not applicable in sovereign gold bonds. Physical gold has other costs such as making charges and cost of bank lockers to store it safely.

- **Real estate** is another common investment avenue but needs very high amounts of investment, typically 50 lakhs to 1 crore for flats and more for land.

  It is better to invest with famous and established builders since their flats will have a better resale value, and in land to invest with municipal authorities in new layouts such as Delhi Development Authority or DDA.

  Another low-cost way for property is to invest in Real estate investment trusts (REITs) or fractional ownership of office space. Examples of REITs whose shares can be traded in the Indian stock markets include Embassy REIT and Mindspace REIT.

- Another option is to invest in **fixed deposits or FDs** with the bank. FDs are usually very safe, have a better interest rate than savings account, but one's money is locked up for the duration of the FD which may be 6 months to a few years. FDs can be offered by one's own bank, such as state bank of India, or by other financial institutions such as Bajaj Capital.

Also, they may have not so high interest rates when compared to inflation, and the interest given is subject to income tax at one's normal tax slab. One may opt for monthly or periodic interest payouts or interest payout at maturity.

Senior citizens typically get better rates in FDs. Recently, many FDs have been giving better rates up to 8.5 or 9% for senior citizens and slightly less for others.

- It is important to save money in the longer term, for one's **retirement**. For this, many people have **Employees Provident Fund** or EPF provided by their employers at the place they work, which gives interest of around 8%. Another option is **Public Provident Fund** or PPF, which is safe and currently gives around 7% interest, which is usually for 15 years but may be extended longer. These investments are beneficial for tax, most of them are claimable tax free under section 80C of the Income Tax. Another option for retirement is **National Pension Scheme or NPS**, which has two tiers: tier 1 NPS is tax free, but money cannot be withdrawn until one is 60 years of age. ELSS is another tax saving scheme one can use to invest in mutual funds, although one must stay invested for a minimum of 3 years.

- One should also have some form of insurance, to cover unfortunate events such as medical emergencies and death. These include various forms such as **term insurance** (pays out an amount on death of the policyholder), **health**

insurance (pays an amount on hospitalization and medical treatments)**, life insurance** (pay out an amount on death as well as some money on maturity) and **Unit Linked Insurance Plans** or **ULIPs.** Here too there is a wide choice of insurance companies such as Life Insurance Corporation of India, ICICI Direct, Tata AIG, HDFC Ergo, Niva Bupa or Max Bupa, Navi etc. Ditto from Zerodha and others are insurance advisors who can give advice on comparing and choosing between different insurance schemes.

- Other ways to invest include alternative investments, such as **P2P lending** (such as indiap2p.com IndiaP2P or 12% club), agriculture (growpital.com), green investments (such as sustvest.com), fractional shares in company property, tykeinvest.com for investing in startups, unlisted shares, movie audio and video rights and so on.

- PMS or **Portfolio Management Services** (sites such as pmsbazaar.com or Dezerv.in) claim to give better returns than mutual funds, but may have higher fees and a higher minimum capital requirement such as minimum investment of 50 lakh rupees. AI based or manual robo-advisors such as TejiMandi and Jarvis also have services, where they give suggestions on when to buy and sell some chosen stocks to generate maximum profit, for a fixed fee.

- Another new way to invest is in **cryptocurrency** such as Bitcoin and Ethereum and Dogecoin and SHIB coin (available in India from platforms such as WazirX and Coinswitch Kuber).

- More risky and modern ways to invest include **derivatives, forex and commodity trading**. Trading in alternative investments can give faster returns but can also cause bigger losses faster, one should only go for trading if they are willing to invest the time and have the appropriate risk profile and enough training.

One should also think of setting a goal of a corpus to achieve as a result of their investment, such as minimum Rupees 1 to 1.5 crore after 10 to 15 years. Then one should calculate how much to invest every month or every year based on their goal and expected returns. The formula to use is $PV = FV/(1 + i)^n$ where PV = present value, FV = future value, i = decimalized interest rate, and n = number of periods.

4.2 Books and resources about money management and investing

It is always better to first learn about investing from books and training courses in YouTube and apps and websites like Investopedia. One should be familiar with the terms by reading financial sections of newspapers and magazines.

There are a number of good **YouTube channels** related to trading and investing in India. Examples include Sunil Miglani, Trade Brains, Pranjal Kamra, Finnovation Z, Groww, Trading Chanakya, Asset Yogi, Fund Guruji, Learn to Invest, Super Trader Lakshya, Market Maestroo, etc. Some of these may not be suitable for beginners, so one can try an episode and subscribe to those channels which they can understand and are useful.

There are also some good **apps** to learn about the stock market, trading and investments such as Siyona Training academy (good for beginners), investing game, Learn: stock market investing and Cashflow game, Varsity by Zerodha and so on.

Some good **newspapers** include Economic Times, Mint, Hindu Businessline, Financial express, Financial chronicle, Business Standard, Financial times (from UK), Economic Times, Magazines include Outlook money, Capital Market, Dalal Street Investment Journal, Forbes India, Business Today, Businessworld, Business India, the Economist (from UK).

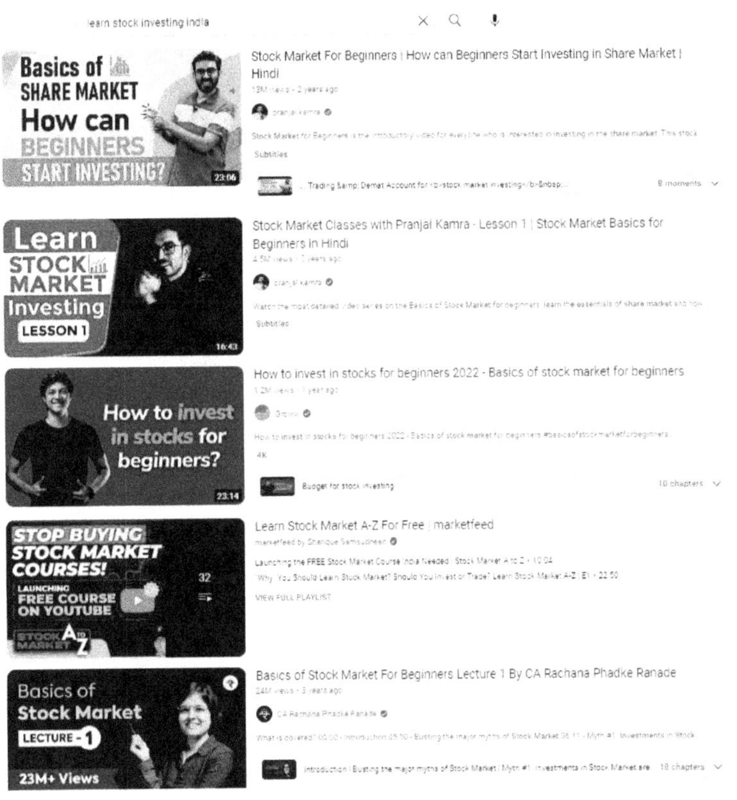

Figure: Screenshot of some YouTube channels to learn stock investing in India

Figure: Screenshot of some good books related to investing and trading

Some good books about money management include:

- The psychology of money by Morgan Housel

- Money master the game by Tony Robbins

- Rich dad poor dad by Robert Kiyosaki

- Smart Money Moves by Vinod Desai

- The Bee, The Beetle, & the Money Bug – The BankBazaar Guide to the Financial Wild by Adhil Shetty

- All about money by Simon Daniel

- The Psychology of Money by Morgan Housel

Some good books about investing include:

- The intelligent investor by Benjamin Graham

- Stocks to Riches by Parag Parikh

- Fundamental analysis for investors by Raghu Palat

- Rakesh Jhunjhunwala How To Make Money in Stock Market

- Investing 101 by Michele Cagan

- The little book that beats the market by Joel Greenblatt

- The little book of behavioral investing by James Montier

- The intelligent asset allocator by William Bernstein

- Coffee Can Investing by Saurabh Mukherjea and Rakshit Ranjan

- Unshakable by Tony Robbins

- The Motley Fool investment guide by David and Tom Gardner

- One up on Wall Street by Peter Lynch

- The four pillars of investing by William Bernstein

- The Bogleheads guide to investing by John C Bogle

- Investment Advisor (Level 1 and Level 2) by NISM

- The Warren Buffett Way by Robert Hagstrom

- The intelligent asset allocator by William Bernstein

Some books about trading include:

- Technical analysis of the financial markets by John Murphy

- Reminiscences of a stock operator by Edwin Lefevre

- How to make money trading with candlestick charts by Balkrishna Sadekar

- Cashtags by Vishal and Meghana Malkan

4.3 Some principles to identify good companies to invest

Warren Buffet and Benjamin Graham were advocates of an actively managed stock investing strategy. As per their philosophy, it is better to do .proper and thorough research to find the best undervalued stocks that are likely to generate good profits in the long term, rather than the short term.

Some of the important ratios related to fundamental analysis to identify good stocks include the following:

- **Price Per Earnings ratio or P/E ratio**: This is the stock price divided by Earnings per share. This should not be too high relative to other companies in the same sector. A lower PE ratio indicates that the stock represents good value, since its price is not too high compared with the earnings.

- **Dividend Yield**: This is the dividends per share divided by the stock price. A higher dividend yield is better and it should be consistent over the last few years. A good company is one that regularly pays dividends.

- **Debt to Equity ratio or DE ratio** shows how much debt a company has compared to its assets. A lower DE ratio is better.

- **ROI or return on Investment (along with ROCE or return on capital employed)**: These are measures of how profitable the company is, a higher ROI and ROCE is better.

- **Enterprise Value-to-EBITDA (EV/EBITDA) Ratio**: This measures the company's market value relative to its earnings before interest, taxes, depreciation, and amortization. A lower value for this ratio is better.

- **Market cap**: Companies that have a bigger market cap are more likely to be stable and produce regular dividends.

- **Piotroski score**: this is a formula that reflects how much financially strong the company is, a score of at least 7 or 8 or above is better.

One can compare these ratios for different companies to see which one is better. Also, one can put the formula for these ratios in screener.in (or readymade screeners in tickertape.in) to get a list of companies that match the criteria. After that one can read up and do additional research on the companies. It is good to also read up about the company and sector, the general news and specific recent news about the management, understand the unique selling point or USP of the company relative to its competitors.

After one has identified a company to invest using fundamental analysis, one can then use technical analysis to understand the best time to invest in it. Technical analysis involves reading the historical graph of the share price going up or down within last few days or months, and identifying patterns based on its price movements such as candlesticks. Technical analysis techniques are used heavily by day traders to identify when to buy and when to sell a stock.

However, it is better to spend good time in identifying the best stocks and buy a stock for the long term, at least a few years, rather than short term. One should also do a periodic review of their investments from time to time and be ready to sell at the right time.

4.4 Conclusion

In this chapter we have gone through some basic principles of investing in India. Beginners to investing should make a good effort to gain as much knowledge as possible for a few months from different books and other sources before seriously starting to invest. Having a mentor to help with good investing advice is also a useful idea.

Chapter 5: How to search for ethical investing opportunities

In this chapter, we discuss some ways to search and find possible avenues for ethical investing.

5.1 Places to search for ethical funds and stocks

Ethical companies and funds can be searched in the following places (India-specific):

- Money and investing websites such as moneycontrol, cleartax or yahoo finance

- Search engines such as Google or Bing or ChatGPT

- Broker websites such as zerodha, indmoney, sharekhan, 5paisa, upstoxx, icici direct or groww

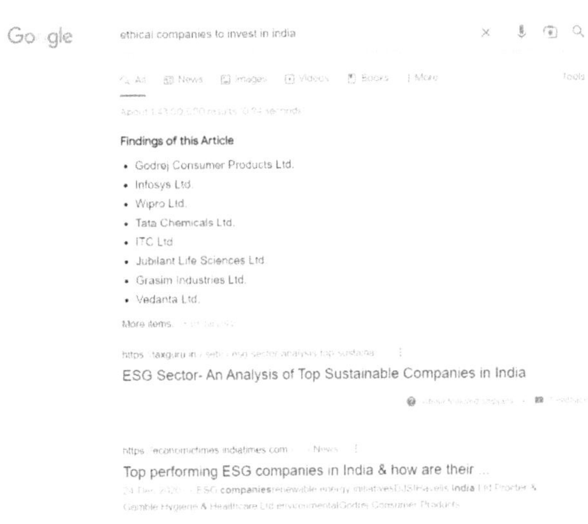

Figure: Screenshot of google to search for ethical companies to invest in India.

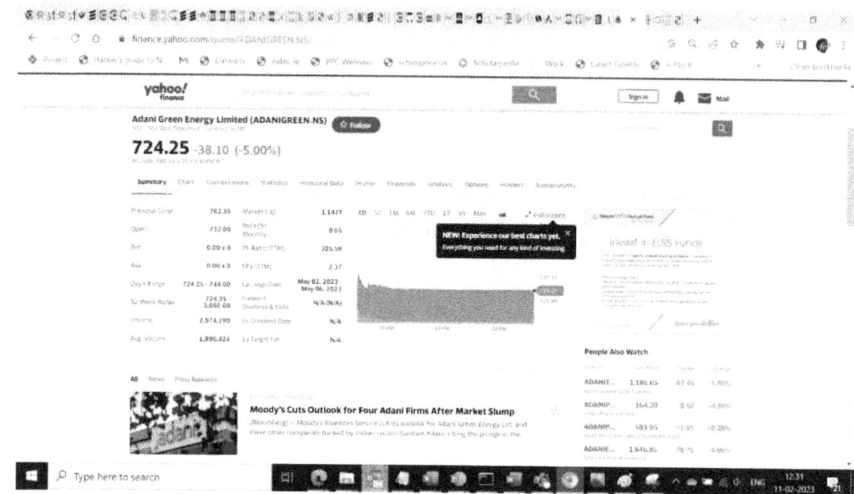

Figure: Screenshot showing analysis of a green firm on yahoo finance.

5.2 Money and investing websites

These include websites such as moneycontrol, yahoo finance, google finance etc. We can use such websites to keep track of the ESG and ethical related stocks and funds and also track the metrics such as P/E ratio, debt to equity and RoI, to decide whether the stock or fund is worth investing.

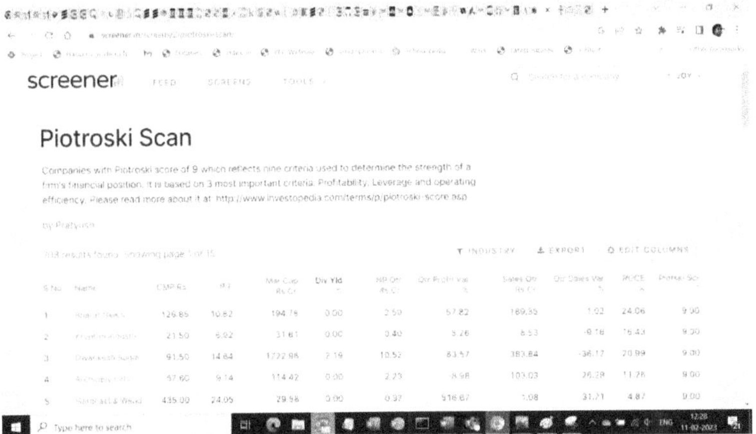

Figure: Screenshot of screener.in showing a screener that can be used to screen stocks as per some criteria or screening formulas based on metrics such as PE or ROI or dividend etc

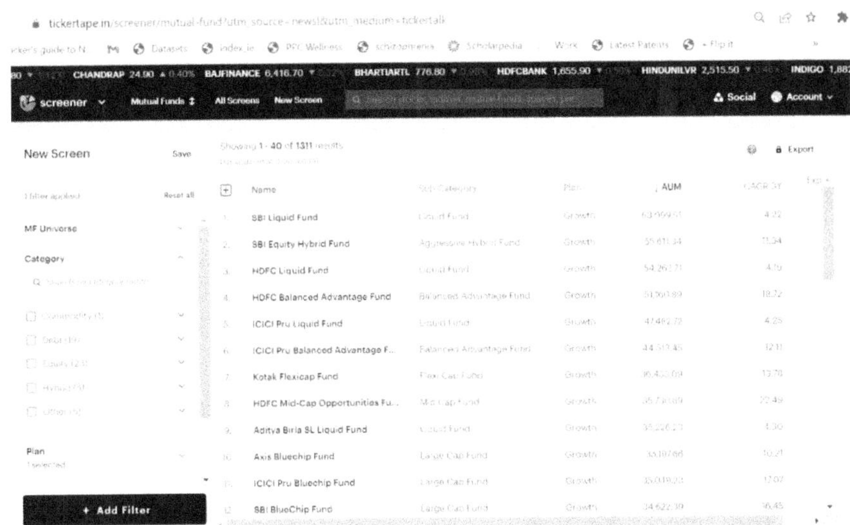

Figure: Screenshot of a screener in tickertape.in

We can also use screeners such as screener.in and tickertape.in for the same purpose.

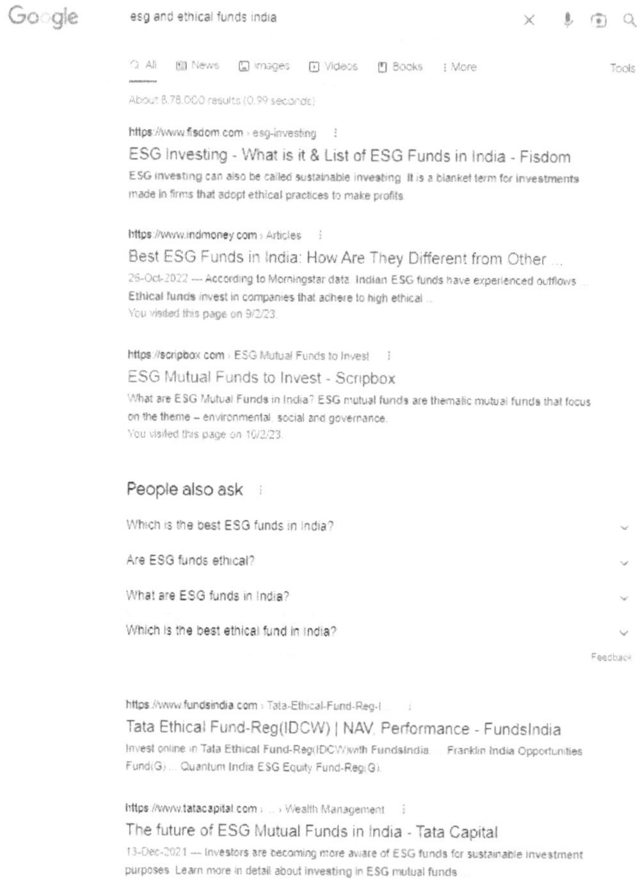

Figure: Search results on google for ESG and ethical funds.

5.3 Search engines

We can search for ethical investing in search engines like google or bing by searching for keywords relevant to ethical investing, such as "esg", "shariah" or "ethical".

Another option is to ask AI chatbots such as ChatGPT for questions related to ethical investing.

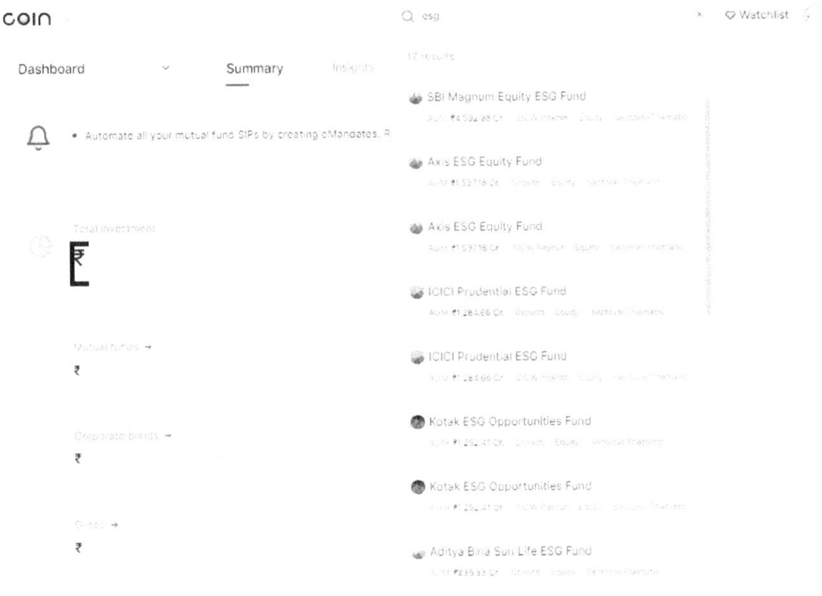

Figure: Screenshot of Zerodha coin showing the ESG mutual funds

5.4 Broker websites

Broker websites such as zerodha, groww, indmoney, ICICI direct or sharekhan can be similarly used to search for ESG or ethical funds and also analyze their performance.

5.5 Conclusion

In this chapter, we discussed some of the sources where we can get more information about ethical investing related funds and stock performance.

Chapter 6: Investing in Green Energy

In this chapter, we discuss some avenues for investing in green energy in India. Green energy is currently a major growth sector due to various incentives and tax concessions given by the government of India to this sector.

6.1 What are the investing avenues related to green energy

The main avenues related to green energy are as follows:

- Green stocks

- Green energy smallcases

- Sovereign Green bonds

- Fractional ownership of green assets

6.2 Green stocks

Green stocks and funds avoid companies that are related to pollution and include those companies that invest in green energy, clean water and other environmental causes.

Example: Adani Green Energy, https://www.adanigreenenergy.com/ which is a company focused on renewable green energy and operates large solar and wind farm projects.

Some listed companies in the Indian stock market (BSE and NSE) investing in renewable energy sources and other environment friendly practices include the following:

- Adani Green Energy

- Borosil Renewables: invests in renewable energy

- GAIL (India): invests in solar energy

- Indian Oil Corporation: invests in renewable energy

- JSW Energy: invests in renewable energy, mainly solar and wind projects

- Larsen & Toubro

- NTPC

- Reliance Industries: invests in renewable energy

- Tata Power Company

- Websol Energy System

- Suzlon energy

- Praj industries

- Gravita

- VaTech Wabag: related to water treatment

- Torrent power: is a power generation company that is investing in renewable energy

- GSPL

- IGL

- Ion exchange: water and waste management company

- Havells India Ltd (part of the Dow Jones sustainability index)

- Godrej consumer products (part of the Dow Jones sustainability index)

- Nestle India: has multiple sustainable projects

- P&G Hygiene & Healthcare: follows environmentally sustainable and socially responsible practices

- Colgate Palmolive India: has a variety of social projects with NGOs

- Page industries: has a sustainability culture

References:

https://www.equitymaster.com/detail.asp?date=12/09/2021&story=5&title=Indias-Top-Renewal-Energy-Stocks-Big-Returns-or-Boring-Returns

https://changestarted.com/green-companies-in-india-that-are-listed-on-stock-exchange/

https://www.ndtv.com/business/top-4-esg-stocks-to-add-to-your-watchlist-2699714

6.3 Green Energy smallcases

Another example is Green Energy related smallcases, which includes a basket of companies that are related to Green Energy. These can be searched in www.smallcase.com website. This is a portfolio of stocks, which will get benefit from the energy transition.

Energy transition refers to the global energy sector's shift from fossil-based systems of energy production and consumption —

including oil, natural gas, and coal — to renewable energy sources like wind and solar, as well as other sources like biofuels.

Their major investment rationale is as follows:

Things like solar panel installations, electric vehicle sales are at record highs. ESG factors in Investing – Due to ESG factors in Investing, the energy transition will continue to increase in importance. Renewable electricity is increasingly cheaper than any new power capacity based on fossil fuels, according to a report by the International Renewable Energy Agency (IRENA). Climate change is set to be one of the top priorities for the world. More than a hundred countries have joined an alliance aiming for net-zero emissions by 2050.

The links are as follows, or else one can search for green energy in smallcase.com:

https://www.smallcase.com/smallcase/green-energy-portfolio-NIVTR_0001

https://www.smallcase.com/smallcase/green-energy-CHTSMO_0036

6.4 Sovereign Green Bonds (SGB)

The Government of India's Sovereign Green Bonds is another good way to invest in environment friendly initiatives by the government of India. These were introduced in the 2022-23 budget with the note *"As a part of the government's overall market borrowings in 2022-23, sovereign Green Bonds will be issued for mobilizing resources for green infrastructure. The proceeds will be deployed in public sector projects which help in reducing the carbon intensity of the economy."*

The aim of the SGB bond is to help in achieving India's green goals. These include five nectar elements (Panchamrit) of India's climate action: 1) Reach 500GW non-fossil energy capacity by 2030 2) 50 per cent of its energy requirements from renewable energy by 2030 3) Reduction of total projected carbon emissions by one billion tonnes from now to 2030 4) Reduction of the carbon intensity of the economy by 45 per cent by 2030, over 2005 levels 5) Achieving the target of net zero emissions by 2070.

The primary SGB bonds can be bought from RBI retail direct once they are issued (one announcement for their issuance was done in Jan 2023), from brokers such as zerodha or groww. They are usually sold in batches of 10, costing around Rupees 10000. They can also be bought in the secondary market from the brokers websites. Investment in these SGB bonds is usually low risk since they are guaranteed by the government.

Reference:
https://www.rbi.org.in/Scripts/BS_PressReleaseDisplay.aspx?prid =55164

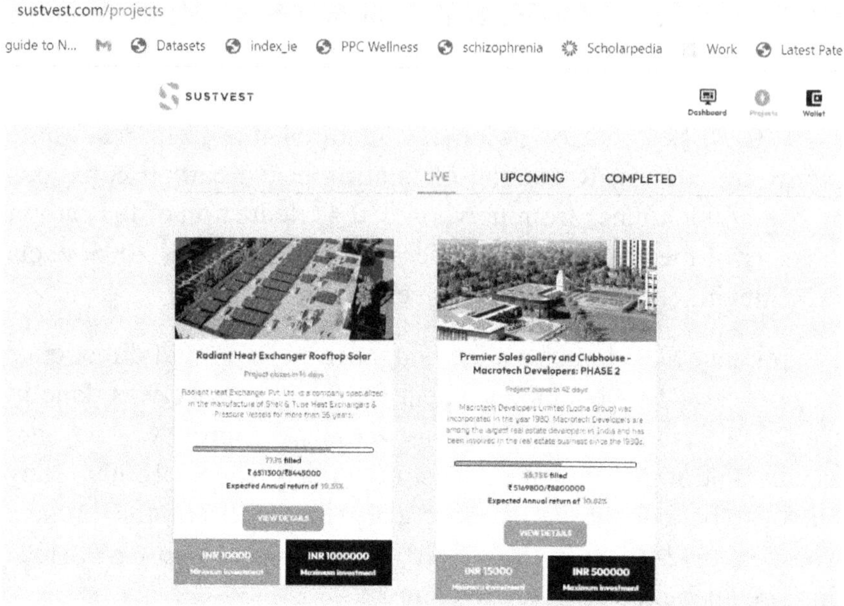

Figure: Screenshot of green energy projects such as project on solar energy panels, in sustvest.com website with the minimum investment

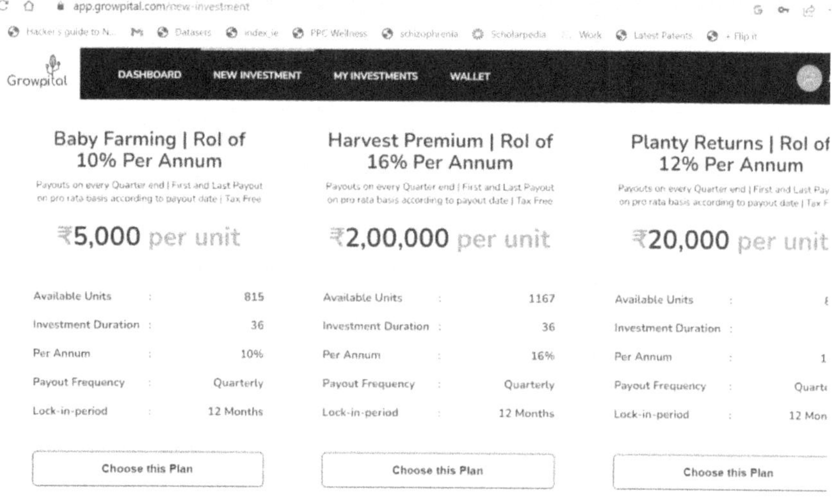

Figure: Screenshot of growpital website showing options for agricultural investing, each with its own minimum investment and lock in period

6.5 Fractional ownership of green assets

Another option is fractional ownership of Green assets. There are a few small companies working in the area that facilitate investments.

These include the following, besides others:

- Sustvest, which has multiple projects related to sustainability such as solar energy, where the investors can invest from as little as 5K or 10K rupees or higher. The website is https://www.sustvest.com/

- Growpital https://growpital.com/ helps in making agricultural investments which can then be claimed tax free as per section 10(1) of the income tax act.

Since green energy is a growing theme in India, one can find many startups also coming up on the theme of green energy and sustainability. For startups, one may search opportunities for investing in tykeinvest.com. There may be new companies coming up with IPOs as well.

6.6 Conclusion

In this chapter we have discussed about green energy and its various investment avenues in India.

Chapter 7: Social Investing

In this chapter we discuss socially responsible investing or social investing. These are microcredit websites that invest in villages and low-income communities, who often suffer from the problem of high interest loan sharks and moneylenders.

7.1 RangDe

Social investing is involved in empowering communities. Rang De is one of the leading platforms for social investing in India. Its website is https://rangde.in/ RangDe lends affordable loans to farmers, artisans and entrepreneurs, and in investing in it one can enable social progress as well as earn returns.

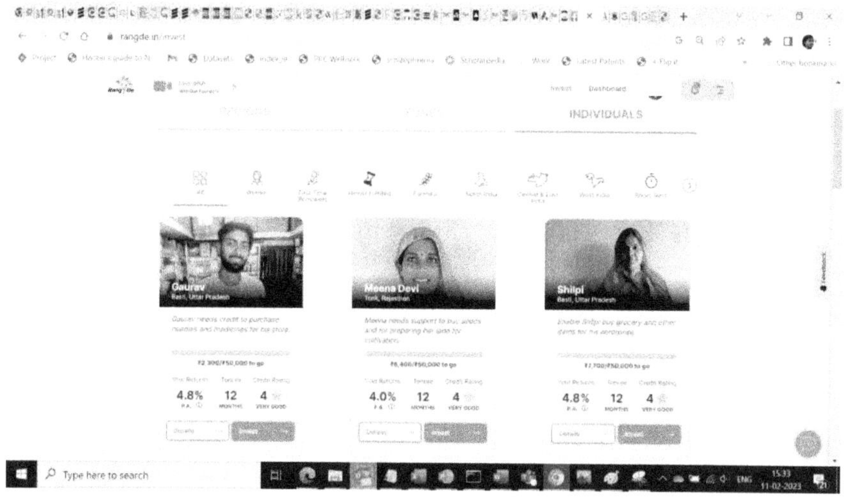

Figure: Screenshot of the RangDe website showing people from villages in different parts of India who need financing at a good interest rate for their small businesses.

7.2 International Microfinance platforms for social projects

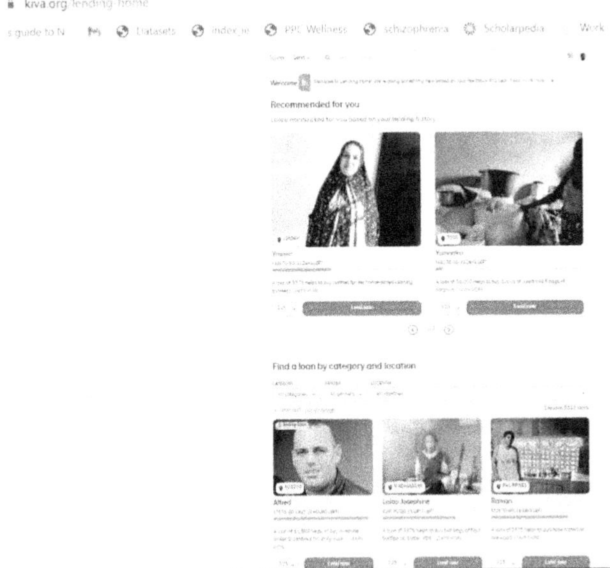

Figure: Screenshot of the kiva website showing available needs for microfinance lending

There are also a few foreign financing websites which include Indian projects such as kiva and lendwithcare.

The Kiva website www.kiva.org has a number of projects all over the world in different areas such as agriculture, education, food, health etc. However, kiva is based in the US. One can pay into the kiva.org website via paypal.

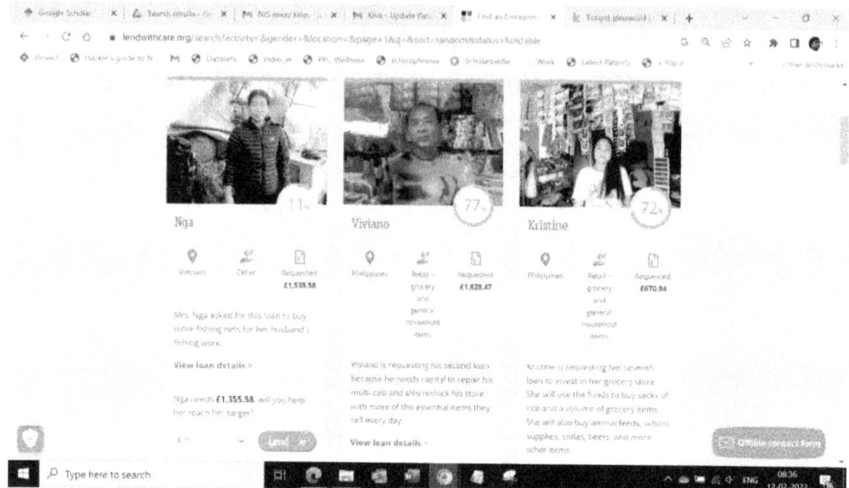

Figure: Screenshot of the lendwithcare website showing available needs for microfinance lending

The Lendwithcare website https://lendwithcare.org/ is a UK based website similar to RangDe and Kiva. It too sponsors social projects all over the world.

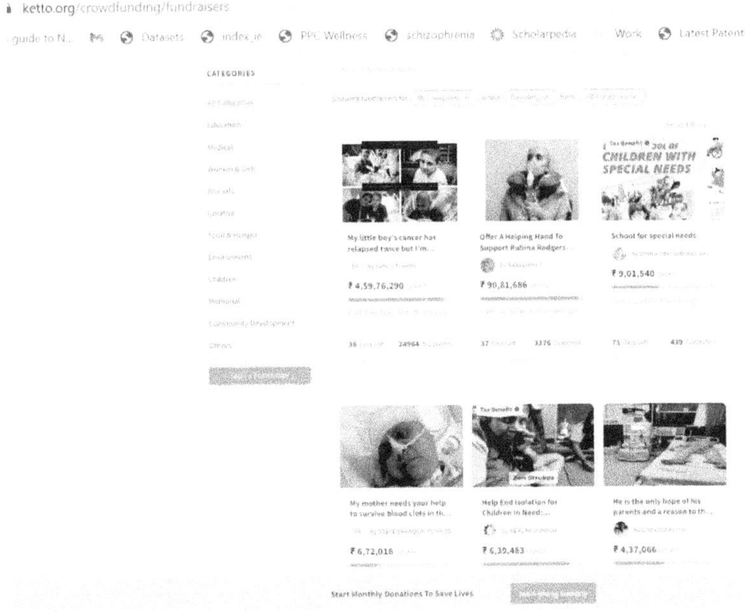

Figure: Screenshot of the Ketto website showing the currently running medical fundraisers.

7.3 Other social fundraising platforms based in India

There are a number of microfinance platforms and websites, as well as charities, which work in the development area and where one can invest or give directly. Donations to registered charities can be claimed against income tax section 80G.

Some of these include the following:

- Ketto: for medical fundraising, meeting medical bills of needy people. https://www.ketto.org/

- Milaap: Also for medical fundraising. https://milaap.org/crowdfunding/fundraisers

- Give.do: For donating and fundraising for various needy people and causes. https://give.do/

- Social for Action: Fundraising site https://socialforaction.com/

- Akshayapatra foundation: for donating meals to children and others https://www.akshayapatra.org/

7.4 Conclusion

In this chapter, we have discussed social investing and fundraising platforms including rangde.in and others.

Chapter 8: Investing in environmental, social, and governance (ESG) mutual funds

In this chapter, we discuss some ESG funds which the interested investor can examine and invest in.

8.1 ESG criteria

The environmental social and governance (ESG) criteria include the company's culture, risk appetite and management. They include environmental, social, and governance standards. The company needs to be environment-friendly in their operations, ethical in its financial disclosures and can sustain the highest governance standards to be included under the criteria.

- **Environmental criteria** may include factors such as the carbon footprint, resource usage, waste management, and efforts to mitigate climate change by the company.

- **Social criteria** may include factors such as labor practices, diversity and inclusion policies, and human rights record of the company.

- **Governance criteria** may include factors such as the company's board diversity, executive compensation structure, and transparency in financial reporting.

For example, for the SBI Magnum Equity ESG Fund, the companies meeting the ESG criteria include the following:

- Housing Development Finance Corporation Ltd.

- ICICI Bank Ltd.

- HDFC Bank Ltd.

- Infosys Ltd.

- Axis Bank Ltd.

- Larsen & Toubro Ltd.

- Ultratech Cement Ltd.

- State Bank of India

- Mahindra & Mahindra Ltd.

- Kotak Mahindra Bank Ltd.

- Britannia Industries Ltd.

- Maruti Suzuki India Ltd.

- Eicher Motors Ltd.

- Tata Consultancy Services Ltd.

8.2 List of ESG mutual funds

There are a number of mutual funds that are focused on ESG criteria companies and are usually identified with the term ESG in their title or description. These can be invested through any of the stock brokers or also from the netbanking sites of most banks like Kotak, SBI and ICICI.

A list of ESG mutual funds available for investors in India is as follows:

- **SBI Magnum Equity ESG Fund**: https://www.sbimf.com/sbimf-scheme-details/SBI-Magnum-Equity-ESG-Fund-1 invests mainly in companies that follow good ESG practices. An open-ended Equity scheme investing in companies following the EGS theme.

- **Axis ESG Equity Fund** https://www.axismf.com/mutual-funds/equity-funds/axis-esg-equity-fund/ee-gp/regular An Open-ended equity scheme investing in companies demonstrating sustainable practices across Environment, Social and Governance (ESG) theme

- **ICICI Prudential ESG Fund** https://www.icicidirect.com/mutual-funds/nav-details/icici-pru-esg-fund-(g)-41670 This is a fund that encourages Sustainable Investing by investing in Companies that follow the ESG theme.

- **Kotak ESG Opportunities Fund** https://www.kotakmf.com/Products/funds/equity-funds/Kotak-ESG-Opportunities-Fund/Dir-G An Open-ended equity scheme which follows the Environment, Social and Governance (ESG) theme with the flexibility of investing across market capitalization.

- **Aditya Birla Sun Life ESG Fund** https://mutualfund.adityabirlacapital.com/wealth-creation-solutions/aditya-birla-sun-life-esg-fund The objective is to generate long-term capital appreciation by investing in a diversified basket of companies following Environmental, Social and Governance (ESG) theme.

- **Invesco India ESG Equity Fund** https://www.invescomutualfund.com/ This has investments in companies which are selected based on Environmental, Social & Governance (ESG) criteria.

- **Quant ESG Equity Fund** https://quantmutual.com/equity/quant-esg-equity-fund This fund has the objective to generate long term capital appreciation by investing in a diversified portfolio of companies demonstrating sustainable practices across Environmental, Social and Governance (ESG) parameters.

- **Quantum India ESG Equity Fund** https://www.quantumamc.com/equity-funds/quantum-india-esg-equity-fund The Quantum India ESG Equity Fund invests in companies that are focused on conserving the environment, on positively impacting communities that they operate in, and conducting business ethically. These sustainable businesses are not only environmentally and socially responsible but also make great sense as investments as you look to build wealth over the long term.

- **Mirae Asset Nifty 100 ESG Sector Leaders Fund of Fund** https://www.miraeassetmf.co.in/mutual-fund-scheme/fof-and-index-funds/mirae-asset-nifty-100-esg-sector-leaders-fund-of-fund As per investment objective, the scheme will predominantly invest in units of Mirae Asset ESG Sector Leaders ETF, the portfolio of which shall mostly be based on stocks forming part of Nifty100 ESG Sector Leaders Index.

8.3 Conclusion

In this chapter, we have discussed a few types of ESG mutual fund investments.

Chapter 9: Shariah compliant investing

In this chapter we discuss avenues for investing in Shariah compliant funds. These funds are as per certain ethical criteria and open to all for investing, not just Muslims.

9.1 Eligibility criteria for selection of stocks in the Nifty50 Shariah index

The eligibility criteria for selection of stocks for Nifty50 Shariah index includes the following:

- The current constituents of the Nifty 50 index are screened for Shariah compliance, those that are compliant form the Nifty50 Shariah.

- The company should have a listing history of 6 months. A company which comes out with an IPO will be eligible for inclusion in the index, if it fulfills the normal eligibility criteria for the index for a 3 month period instead of a 6 month period.

- Stocks that meet above mentioned criteria and are also Shariah compliant form part of Nifty50 Shariah Index.

- Weightage of each stock in the index is calculated based on its free-float market capitalization such that no single stock shall be more than 33% and weightage of top 3 stocks cumulatively shall not be more than 62% at the time of rebalancing.

These screen stocks with more than a minimum market capitalization where the amount of income from interest, trade receivables and debt is low. The companies should have cash to total assets ratio less than a threshold, debt to company value also less than a threshold (usually 33%), interest income to total income is very low and there is no involvement of the company in weapons, narcotic drugs etc.

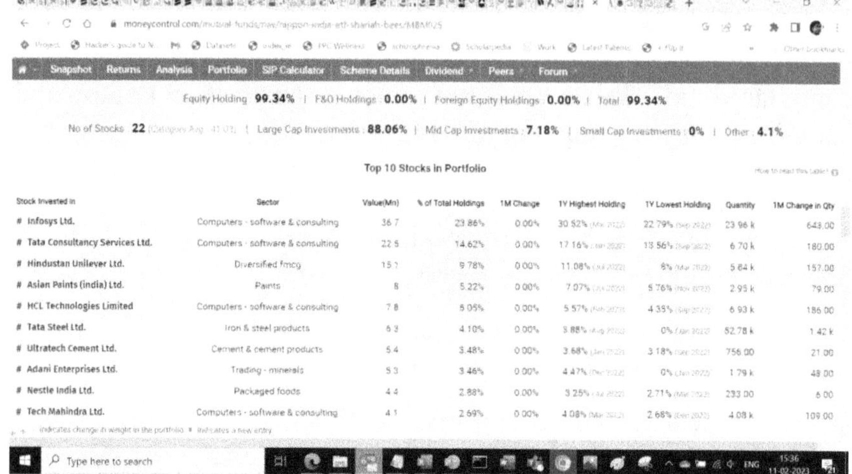

Stock Invested in	Sector	Value(Mn)	% of Total Holdings	1M Change	1Y Highest Holding	1Y Lowest Holding	Quantity	1M Change in Qty
# Infosys Ltd.	Computers - software & consulting	36.7	23.86%	0.00%	30.52% (Mar 2022)	22.79% (Sep 2022)	23.96 k	643.00
# Tata Consultancy Services Ltd.	Computers - software & consulting	22.5	14.62%	0.00%	17.16% (Jan 2022)	13.56% (Sep 2022)	6.70 k	180.00
# Hindustan Unilever Ltd.	Diversified fmcg	15.7	9.78%	0.00%	11.08% (Jul 2022)	8% (Mar 2022)	5.84 k	157.00
# Asian Paints (India) Ltd.	Paints	8	5.22%	0.00%	7.07% (Jul 2022)	5.76% (Nov 2022)	2.95 k	79.00
# HCL Technologies Limited	Computers - software & consulting	7.8	5.05%	0.00%	5.57% (Feb 2022)	4.35% (Sep 2022)	6.93 k	186.00
# Tata Steel Ltd.	Iron & steel products	6.3	4.10%	0.00%	8.88% (Aug 2022)	0% (Jan 2022)	52.78 k	1.42 k
# Ultratech Cement Ltd.	Cement & cement products	5.4	3.48%	0.00%	3.68% (Jan 2022)	3.18% (Sep 2022)	756.00	21.00
# Adani Enterprises Ltd.	Trading - minerals	5.3	3.46%	0.00%	4.47% (Dec 2022)	0% (Jan 2022)	1.79 k	48.00
# Nestle India Ltd.	Packaged foods	4.4	2.88%	0.00%	3.25% (Jul 2022)	2.71% (Mar 2022)	233.00	8.00
# Tech Mahindra Ltd.	Computers - software & consulting	4.1	2.69%	0.00%	4.08% (Mar 2022)	2.68% (Dec 2022)	4.08 k	109.00

Figure: Screenshots from the moneycontrol websites showing some top stocks in the SHARIAHBEES (Nippon India ETF Nifty 50 Shariah Bees) portfolio

9.2 List of Shariah compliant funds

A list of Shariah compliant mutual funds available in India is as follows:

- **Tata Ethical Fund**
  https://www.tatamutualfund.com/products/tata-ethical-fund
  This invests mainly in companies that are Shariah compliant. Tata Ethical Fund is an open-ended equity fund which invests in a diversified equity portfolio based on principles of Shariah. The investment objective of the scheme is to provide medium to long-term capital gains by investing in Shariah compliant equity and equity-related instruments of well-researched value and growth-oriented companies.

- **Nippon India ETF Nifty 50 Shariah BeES**
  https://www.moneycontrol.com/mutual-funds/nav/nippon-india-etf-shariah-bees/MBM025 This ETF (exchange traded fund) invests in companies selected from Nifty50 Shariah Index. The investment objective of Nippon India ETF Nifty 50 Shariah BeES (Formerly Nippon India ETF Shariah BeES) is to provide returns that, before expenses, closely correspond to the total returns of the Securities as represented by the Nifty50 Shariah Index by investing in Securities which are constituents of the Nifty50 Shariah Index in the same proportion as in the Index.

- **Taurus ethical fund**
  https://www.taurusmutualfund.com/taurus-ethical-fund
  This is a Shariah compliant fund. Investors looking for suitable investment opportunities that comply with Shariah norms should look to invest in the Taurus Ethical fund with a Medium to Long term investment horizon. It is a socially responsible form of investing. It is a suitable form of S&P BSE 500 Shariah Index will be used as the benchmark for comparing the performance of this Scheme.

9.3 Conclusion

In this chapter we have considered avenues for Shariah compliant investing.

Chapter 10: Wellness related companies and funds listed on NSE and BSE

In this chapter we look at some wellness related companies that are listed in BSE And NSE. Wellness may be considered as a part of ethical investing since it is related to overall well-being.

10.1 Listed wellness related companies

Some of the wellness related companies listed in NSE and BSE include the following:

- **Dabur India**: Dabur is one of the best known ayurvedic brands in India. It was set up in 1884. It manufactures a number of products including Dabur Chyawanprash. Its website is https://www.dabur.com/

- **Patanjali**: It is an ayurveda company under yoga guru Baba Ramdev. It manufactures a range of affordable ayurveda related products. Its website is https://www.patanjaliayurved.net/

- **Zydus Wellness**: It produces health food products, skincare and other wellness related products including well known brands such as Glucon-D, Complan and Nycil. Its website is https://www.zyduswellness.com/

- **Kerala Ayurveda**: It manufactures ayurvedic medicines, has an online ayurvedic store and a number of services such as Vaidya consultations and ayurveda retreats. Its website is https://www.keralaayurveda.biz/

- **Tiaan Consumer** (Tiaan Ayurvedic and He): It is a small cap company that manufactures ayurvedic products. Its website is https://tiaanstore.com/

- **Rajnish Wellness**: It started as a teleshopping venture and grown into a listed company with various wellness products. Its website is https://rajnishwellness.com/

References:

https://vibcare.co.in/top-10-ayurvedic-companies-in-india/

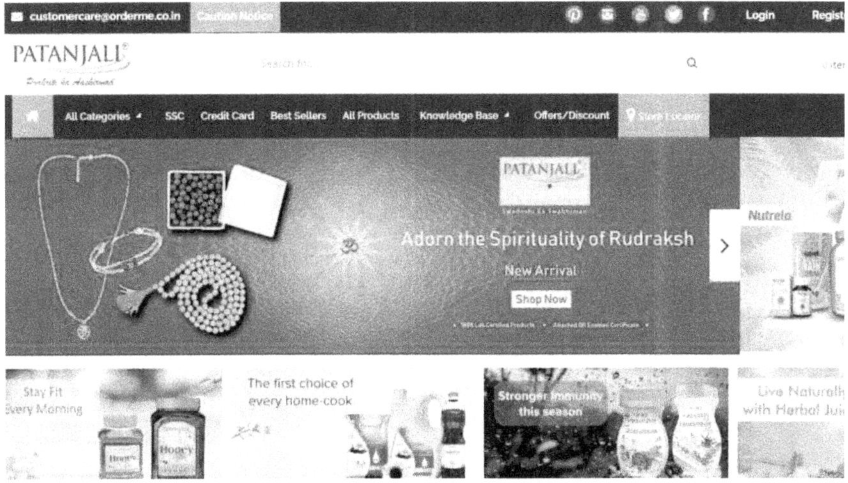

Figure: Screenshot from website of Patanjali ayurveda

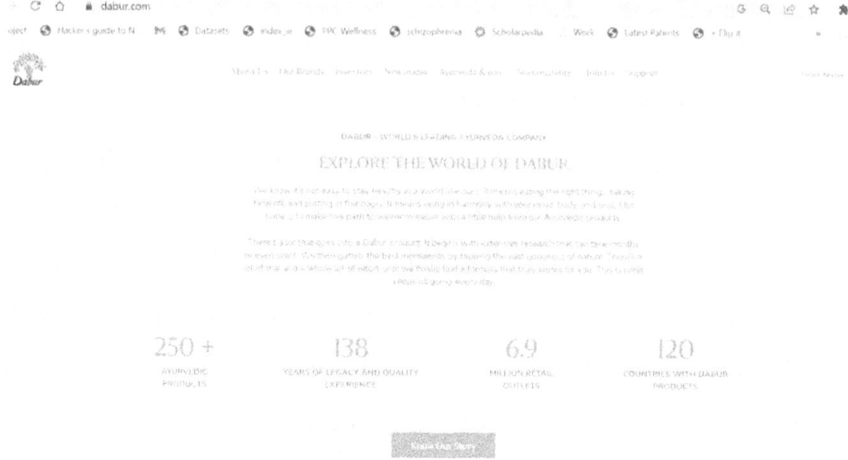

Figure: Screenshot from Dabur website

10.2 Healthcare mutual funds

There are also a few healthcare related mutual funds where one can invest in. Their performance can be tracked by searching for terms such as pharma and healthcare in mutual funds listings at the broker websites such as zerodha.

Some of these include the following:

- SBI Healthcare opportunities fund

- UTI healthcare fund

- Tata India Pharma and healthcare fund

- Nippon India Pharma fund

- DSP healthcare fund

- UTI healthcare fund

- ICICI Prudential Pharma Healthcare and Diagnostics (P.H.D) Fund

- Mirae Asset healthcare fund

- Aditya Birla Sun Life Pharma & Healthcare Fund

- IDBI healthcare fund

10.3 Conclusion

In this chapter, we have discussed a few wellness, ayurveda and nutrition related companies and mutual funds listed on the Indian stock market.

Chapter 11: Conclusion

In this book, we have briefly discussed the meaning of ethical investing and explored some of the investment avenues in India where one can invest ethically.

Ethical investing is only one part of a lifestyle that displays a healthy relationship with money, as a means of exchanging positive energy with the people around us, so that we can contribute to building a better world for everyone. Investing in ESG and ethical funds and social investing are all steps towards this goal.

If all of us take concrete steps towards ethical investing by doing a periodic ethical audit of our investments and ensuring that we are contributing towards saving rather than destroying this planet, then not only will there be benefits for ourselves and future generations towards building a sustainable and more livable happier world, but the returns we will receive are more likely to be recession proof and positive in the long term.

About the authors

Siva Prasad Bose is an author of introductory guidebooks on aspects of Indian laws. He is currently retired after many years of service as an electrical engineer in Uttar Pradesh Power Corporation Limited. He received his engineering degree from Jadavpur University, Kolkata and has a law degree from Meerut University, Meerut and a BSc from MMH College, Ghaziabad. His interests lie in the fields of family law, civil law, law of contracts, and areas of law related to power electricity related issues. He lives in Delhi.

Joy Bose is a data scientist by profession.

Other Books by Siva Prasad Bose

Introduction to Wills and Probate

Senior Citizens Abuse in India

Introduction to Negotiable Instruments

Introduction to Marriage Laws in India

Neighbor Problems in India and what to do about them

Delays in Court Cases in India

Self-Publish Books and E-Books in India

Introduction to Patents and Patent Law in India

Introduction to Property Law in India